D1161641

A ROOKIE READER®

GO-WITH WORDS

By Bonnie Dobkin

Illustrated by Tom Dunnington

Prepared under the direction of Robert Hillerich, Ph.D.

CHILDRENS PRESS®

CHICAGO

For the Group: Josh, Jason, Jessica, Elana,
Sara, Jon, Scott, Eric, Ron, and Bradley

Library of Congress Cataloging-in-Publication Data

Dobkin, Bonnie.
  Go-with words / by Bonnie Dobkin ; illustrated by
Tom Dunnington.
      p.   cm. — (A Rookie reader)
  Summary: Rhyming text presents related words,
such as short and long, page and book, and night and
moon.
  ISBN 0-516-02016-1
  1. Vocabulary—juvenile literature. [1. Vocabulary.]
I. Dunnington, Tom, ill. II. Title. III. Series.
PE1449.D63   1993
428.1—dc20   93-13023
                                                         CIP
                                                         AC

Cat goes with kitten.
Dog goes with pup.

Top goes with

bottom.

Down goes with up.

Fat goes with skinny.

Short goes with long.

Read goes with story

and listen with song.

A joke makes you laugh.
A cut makes you cry.

You clap with your hands.
You wink with your eye.

Page goes with book
and brick goes with wall.

Square goes with box
and round goes with ball.

Letters mean reading.

Numbers mean math.

Bad means a time-out.

Dirty means bath.

Night goes with moon

and day goes with sun.

Hand goes in glove,
and hot dog in bun.

A bat hits a ball.

A hammer hits nails.

Trains have cabooses.

Some monkeys have tails.

Eggs go in cartons

and cans on a shelf.

Now think of more go-with
words by yourself.

WORD LIST

a	clap	have	nails	story
and	cry	hits	night	sun
bad	cut	hot dog	now	tails
ball	day	in	numbers	think
bat	dirty	joke	of	time-out
bath	dog	kitten	on	top
book	down	laugh	page	trains
bottom	eggs	letters	pup	up
box	eye	listen	read	wall
brick	fat	long	reading	wink
bun	glove	makes	round	with
by	go	math	shelf	words
cabooses	goes	mean	short	you
cans	go-with	means	skinny	your
cartons	hammer	monkeys	some	yourself
cat	hand	moon	song	
	hands	more	square	

About the Author

Bonnie Dobkin grew up with the last name Bierman in Morton Grove, Illinois. She attended Maine East High School and later received a degree in education from the University of Illinois. A high-school teacher for several years, Bonnie eventually moved into educational publishing and now works as an executive editor. She lives in Arlington Heights, Illinois.

For story ideas, Bonnie relies on her three sons, Bryan, Michael, and Kevin; her husband Jeff, a dentist; and Kelsey, a confused dog of extremely mixed heritage. When not writing, Bonnie focuses on her other interests—music, community theatre, and chocolate.

About the Artist

Tom Dunnington divides his time between book illustrations and wildlife painting. He has done many books for Childrens Press, as well as working on textbooks, and is a regular contributor to "Highlights for Children." Tom lives in Oak Park, Illinois.